# DIM SUM TIME

For our little dumpling Avery.
        XOXOXOXO
    -Mommy and Daddy

每周一次,爸爸和妈妈都会带我,弟弟和姐姐去餐厅吃点心。"吃点心的时间到了!"弟弟大声叫道。

Once a week, mommy and daddy take me, my little brother, and my big sister, to the restaurant for dim sum.

"It's Dim Sum time!" little brother yells out.

有很多点心我喜欢吃，
yǒu hěn duō diǎn xin wǒ xǐ huan chī
但有一个是我最喜
dàn yǒu yī gè shì wǒ zuì xǐ
欢的。
huan de

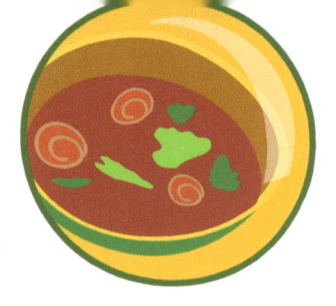

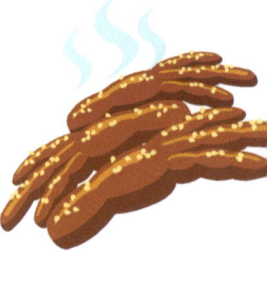

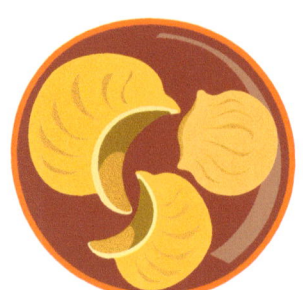

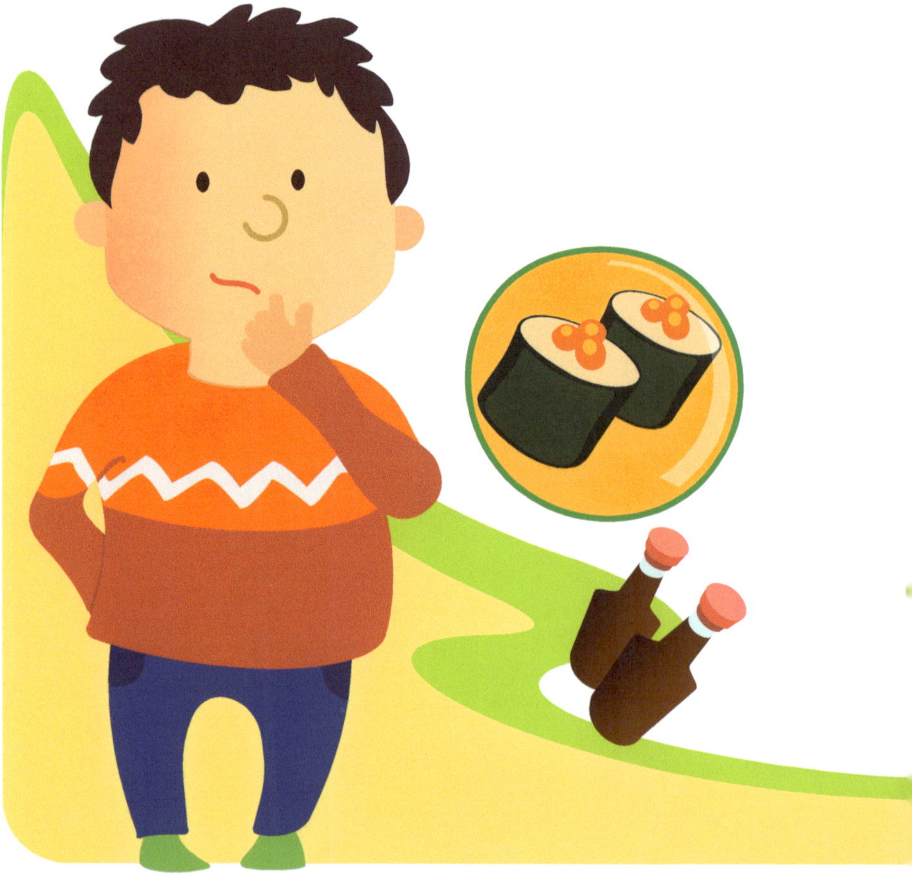

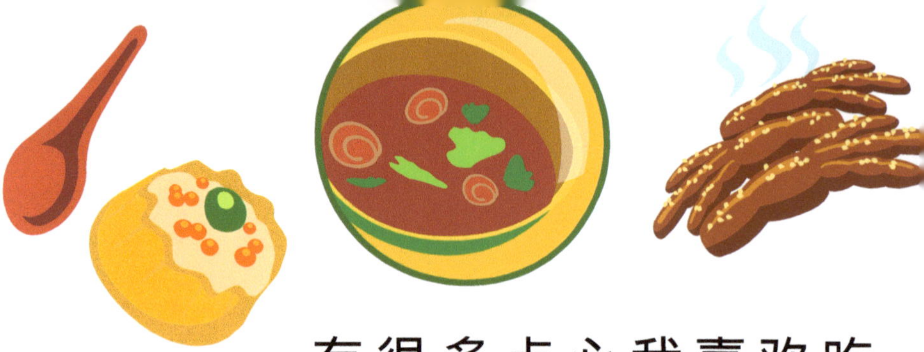

There are lots of dishes that I like, but there's one that is my most favourite of all...

"虾饺!虾饺!我爱虾饺!"
xiā jiǎo　xiā jiǎo　wǒ ài xiā jiǎo

"安静一点吧"妈妈说。
ān jìng yī diǎn bā　mā ma shuì

我告诉肚子要耐心等候.
wǒ gào su dù zi yāo nài xīn děng hòu

"Har gao! Har gao! I love my Har Gao!"

"Hush," says mommy and I tell my tummy to wait.

在餐厅内,服务员推着摆满了
zài cān tīng nèi　　fú wù yuán tuī zhāo bǎi mǎn liǎo

各款点心的小车,一路推一路
gè kuǎn diǎn xin de xiǎo chē　　yī lù tuī yī lù

叫出不同的点心。
jiào chū bù tóng de diǎn xin

有这么多点心,但是我的虾
yǒu zhè me duō diǎn xin　　dàn shì wǒ de xiā

饺在哪里?
jiǎo zài nǎ lǐ

In the restaurant, carts piled high with food are pushed around while waiters call out the dishes.

There are so many dishes to choose from, but where's my Har Gao?

弟弟喜欢叉烧包 - 一个大面包
里装满了美味的肉。
我吃了一个叉烧包,但是我的虾饺在哪里?

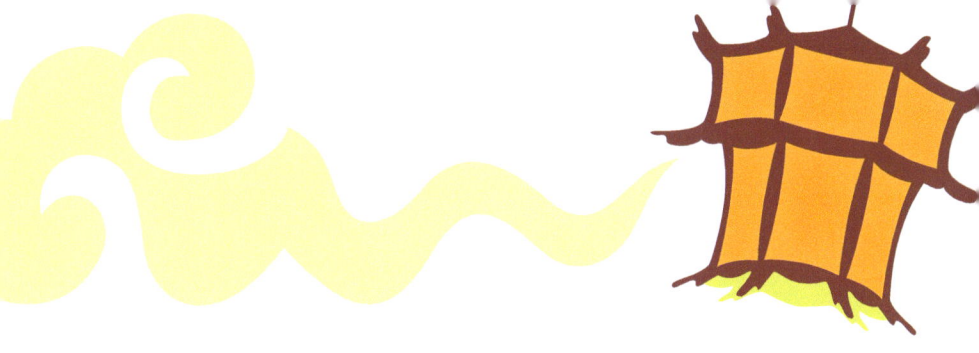

**Little brother likes Char Siu Bao - a fluffy soft bun filled with yummy meat.**

**I eat a Char Siu Bao too, but where's my Har Gao?**

姐姐吃了她喜爱的烧卖 - 薄皮
jiě jie chī liǎo tā xǐ ài de shāo mài　bó pí

里有多汁的猪肉。
lǐ yǒu duō zhī de zhū ròu

我吃了一个烧卖,但是我的虾
wǒ chī liǎo yī gè shāo mài　dàn shì wǒ de xiā

饺在哪里?
jiǎo zài nǎ lǐ

Big sister eats her Siu Mai - juicy pork wrapped in a soft pasta skin.

I eat a Siu Mai too, but where's my Har Gao?

爸爸挑选了他喜爱的凤爪－甜蜜的鸡爪,软滑的皮。
我吃了一只凤爪,但是我的虾饺在哪里?

Daddy picks out his Fong Djau - sweet chicken paws with smooth and soft skin.

I eat a Fong Djau too, but where's my Har Gao?

妈妈订了一些萝卜糕-用萝卜和虾煎炸的食物。

我吃了一块萝卜糕,但是我的虾饺在哪里?

Mommy orders some Loh Bah Go - a fried treat with shrimp and turnip.

I eat a Loh Bah Go too, but where's my Har Gao?

虾饺!虾饺!
xiā jiǎo　xiā jiǎo

我爱虾饺!
wǒ ài xiā jiǎo

Har Gao! Har Gao!
I love my Har Gao!

最后，虾饺终于来了 - 水晶外
zuì hòu xiā jiǎo zhōng yú lái liǎo shuǐ jīng wài

皮里有新鲜的大虾。
pí lǐ yǒu xīn xiān de dà xiā

但是现在我的肚子
dàn shì xiàn zài wǒ de dù zi

已经太饱了。
yǐ jīng tài bǎo liǎo

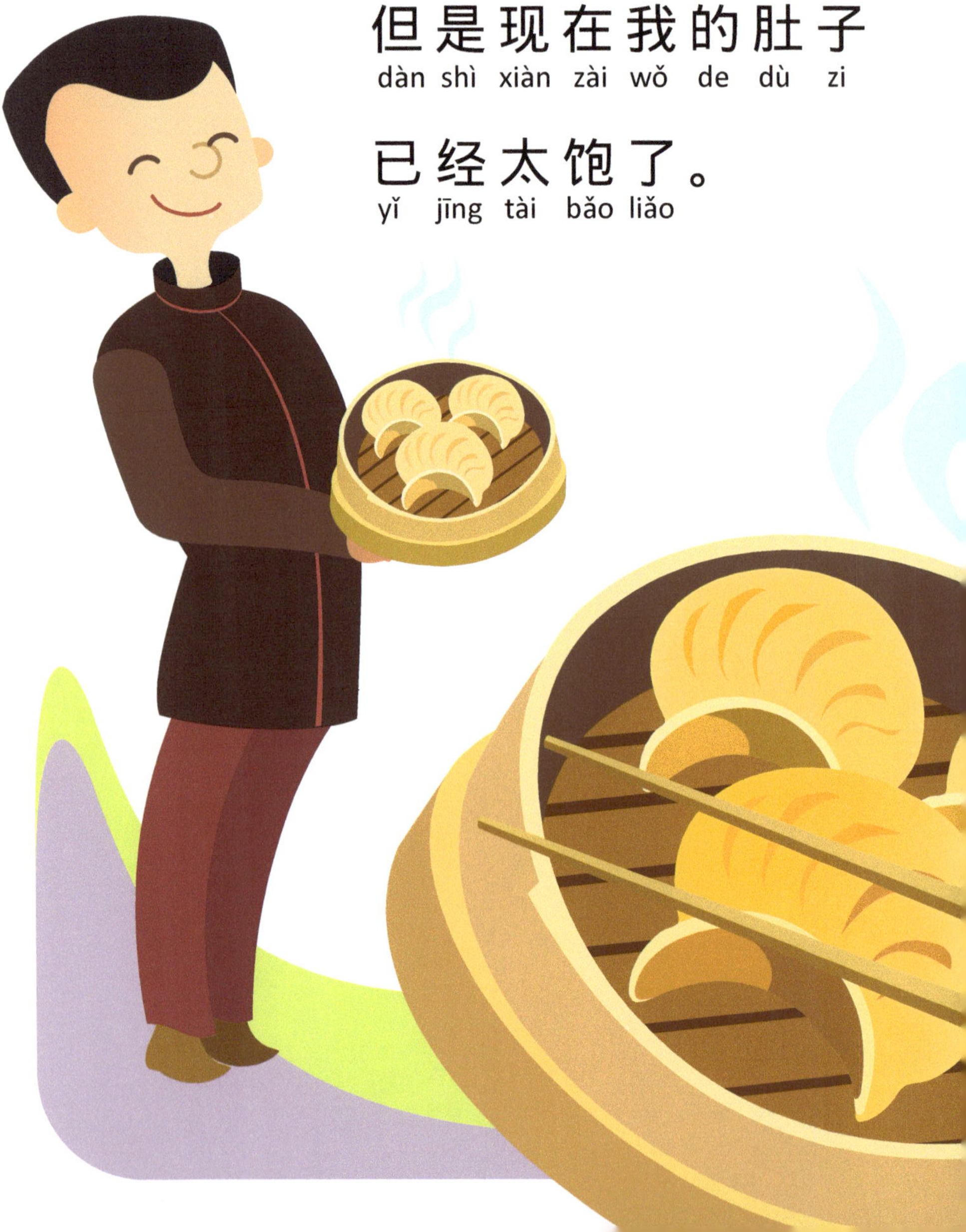

Finally the Har Gao arrives - crystal clear dumpling skin with a big fresh shrimp inside.

But now my tummy is too full.

我请服务员拿一个盒子来打包,把虾饺带回家。

因为我从来不喜欢浪费食物,尤其是…

So I ask the waiter for a box and take the Har Gao's home.

Because I never like to waste food especially when it's ...

虾饺!
xiā jiǎo

虾饺!虾饺!
xiā jiǎo　xiā jiǎo

我爱虾饺!
wǒ ài xiā jiǎo

# Har Gao!

**Har Gao! Har Gao!
I love my Har Gao!**

www.ingramcontent.com/pod-product-compliance
Lightning Source LLC
Chambersburg PA
CBHW041813040426
42450CB00001B/32